EMPOWERING TODAY'S YOUTH SERIES
BOOK ONE

You Have the Power to Create Your World

C. Orville McLeish

You Have the Power to Create Your World.
Copyright © 2018 C. Orville McLeish.
All Rights Reserved.

No rights claimed for public domain material; all rights reserved. No parts of this publication may be reproduced, stored in any retrieval system, or transmitted in any form or by any means, electronic, mechanical, recording, or otherwise, without the prior written permission of the author. Violations may be subject to civil or criminal penalties.

ISBN: 978-1-949343-09-0 (paperback)
978-1-949343-10-6 (ebook)

Printed in the United States of America

To all future world changers and agents of change, may you create a better world for you and those who will come after you than the one we and those before us made for you.

To those who know there is more to life than sex and money.

To those who know they are called to stand out and not fit in.

To those who think there is no place in the world for them.

This book is for YOU!

Table of Contents

Meet The Author 7
Chapter One **19**
   Power to Choose *19*
   Activation *23*
Chapter Two **25**
   Power to Believe *25*
   Activation *28*
Chapter Three **31**
   Power to Speak *31*
   Activation *35*
Chapter Four **39**
   Power to Imagine *39*
   Activation *42*
Chapter Five **45**
   Power to Create *45*
   Activation *48*

Chapter Six **51**
   Power to Feel *51*
   Activation *56*

Chapter Seven **59**
   Power to Know *59*
   Activation *60*

Final Thoughts **63**

Meet The Author

In 1993, I graduated from the St. Jago High School in Spanish Town, St. Catherine, Jamaica, with ZERO passes in the four CXC subjects my parents paid for. I was so sure I was going to fail one of those subjects that I did not bother to take the practical exam. It was not because I was incapable of being an academic genius, but with a consistently bad report falling in my father's hand, I was told I would never amount to anything good; I was worthless, and all I was good for was to burn COAL, and I believed. Children believe everything their parents tell them, so you will understand my concern today when I listen to how parents communicate with their children. By the time we get to our teen years, we have already developed a belief system, and many teenagers believe wholeheartedly that their coming into this world was a mistake and they have no value. It is NOT true.

Parents try to use what is called *"reverse psychology"* in that they will tell you the opposite of what they really want you to believe. I refuse to believe our parents actually believe we are worthless and good for nothing. They say the worst things in trying to get you to be better and good. I don't see the method behind this madness, but that's what parents do.

I didn't grow up in a rich family. My parents could only afford to take us to fifth form in high school, and then we would be on our own. As siblings, we understood this, but not having a clear map for where our lives would go after High School affected us. Maybe we didn't care. So, in 1993, I was out of school, no money, no friends, no qualifications, no dreams and aspirations, and no idea what to do with my life.

My first job was as a SANDER working with my brother who was a carpenter. I sanded furniture from morning to evening. I hated it.

My second job was in my PASTOR'S SUPERMARKET working for $500 (JMD) a week. I hated it.

My third job was as a CEMENT MIXER with my brother who was transitioning from a carpenter to a BUILDING CONTRACTOR. After my first experience 'slabbing' a roof, I knew that was not for me. I hated it. I was destined for failure and a life of hustling, and I knew it. I could not see a way out, nor was I looking for one. I was more than resolved that I was a failure and my life would never have any significance.

Sadly, this path of only being able to do odd jobs is the journey of many youngsters who leave high school. Many teens consume a lot of their time going after the opposite sex and believing that physical, temporary pleasure is the ultimate human experience, but that is NOT true. Most teens also get saved in a church in their early years, but they don't stay as they get older.

I was baptized in my home church, where we grew up, in my late teenage years, maybe 19 years old, but I can't say for sure that I was saved. I was still doing everything I was doing before my baptism and even added some new sins as I entered my 20s.

I remember going to HEART Academy because I had nothing to do. I took a skilled course in carpentry, but I'm not sure why. HEART was a great program that provided work experience when you completed the course, which often led to a permanent job.

While at school, I noticed I was helping students a lot. I was excellent at spelling, and the curriculum seemed to be so far beneath me that I barely paid attention in class and still ended up being the only one who earned the certificate. I didn't bother to collect it. During that time, I kept wondering what I was doing at HEART. I was better than that.

I was sent to a BEDDING Manufacturing Plant to make mattresses for my work experience. I hated it, so I underperformed so they wouldn't keep me on permanently. I always had a problem just doing the same thing repeatedly, every single day. I needed diversity and variety.

My youngest brother, who had dropped out of high school because he liked Mr. Spliff and Wray and his nephew a whole lot more than education, was working with a land surveyor, who happened to also know one of my aunts. They put in a good word that I was smart and had much potential, and I was hired as a trainee surveying draftsman, a trade I knew nothing about. It turned out that they were right about me—I did have potential. I quickly learned the trade, until I was almost senior draftsman with that firm, but the salary was inconsistent, and my boss was constantly under the influence of RUM. After eight years, and a death threat from a drunk boss, I left. I remember praying that God would provide a job that would pay me at least $100,000 (JMD) per month.

Within three weeks, I was hired by another soberer surveyor, and my first drafting assignment was a leg of Highway 2000. During the interview, he mentioned I could make as much as $100,000 (JMD) per month, and I saw that as a confirmation from God, though it took many years before I saw my first check in that amount. I was good with computers. Luckily, to avoid me being too idle a couple summers, Mama sent me to do summer computer courses when the operating system Windows was just coming on the market. So, I have always been good with computers, but I didn't know anything about CAD drafting. I knew how to draw plans manually, but not via computers. I really sucked at using the computer for drafting, and that was required of me on this new job. This is where I began to learn about myself. I would go home and spend my nights teaching myself, then go to work the next day and do my job. I had to spend a lot of time correcting mistakes as well.

Somewhere along my drafting journey, I discovered I could write plays, and I loved it. A PASTOR in Ohio read one of my plays, and he loved it. This was when the INTERNET was coming into the mainstream. The pastor gave me a space on his website for my plays, and I continued to write while working as a full-time surveying draftsman. I was an international playwright, and I didn't even know it. Eventually, I had enough plays to launch out on my own.

In 2002, I realized that the money I was making from writing plays was more than what I was making from my nine-to-five job, so I knew I would one day leave the nine-to-five environment. The day did come. The Survey draughting field was fast becoming extinct, as the new commissioned surveyors coming on the mainstream preferred to do their own plans. They never liked paying draughtsmen anyway.

This is where I started to create my world, without even knowing it. I moved from writing plays to writing movie scripts, but the movie script market was too hard to crack. I entered the JCDC Literary Writing Competition and was awarded every year: gold, silver, bronze medals; trophies and gifts. I got tired of entering because what I really wanted was exposure.

One day God told me to publish a book from some material I had presented at church. That was a shocker. I knew nothing about publishing, but by this time I knew I had a unique gift of understanding enough that I could teach myself anything. I was also very computer literate and knew my way around cyberspace, so with intent research, I discovered self-publishing and taught myself everything there was to learn. I then published my first book. From there, I started writing and publishing my own books, which expanded to writing and publishing books for others, and my world just kept expanding and expanding and expanding.

There are several things I had to learn about myself to achieve what I am going to share with you in this book. Each of you will have a different journey than mine because, along the way, you will have to discover what is in you, and how God or Creation itself is interacting with you to bring you into greatness. You are born to be great. You are born to succeed. But the path reveals itself through knowledge, belief, and application.

These are the qualities I discovered about myself as I journeyed through life:

1. I never resolve that I CANNOT do something, because I am a learning being, which means, I can learn to do everything.
2. I am never too old for school or to learn something new.
3. I have never used a lack of money as an excuse not to accomplish or go after my dreams. I learned that desire always precedes finances. The money always comes.

4. I have never put any limits on myself, because I serve a God WITHOUT limits.

These are my foundations for success. Yours may look a little different, but we all have the potential to be more. If you find yourself living a mediocre life and thinking how worthless and invaluable you are, then that is the world you have created for yourself. The temptation will always be there to think that your life is a result of what people have done to you, but I have written and published too many testimonies to know that your life is the sum total of your *response* to what people do to you and say about you.

Today, I have written for pastors, bishops, evangelists, doctors, nurses, entrepreneurs, businessmen and countless people with a PhD behind their names—well-learned men and women all over the world—and the only subject I have is a pass in Principles of Accounts that I got a couple years after leaving high school. My world should not have been possible for someone like me, but I believe I am an example for many to know that:

1. Success is not always about academic excellence. Education is good, and you should do your best to attain it. It may aid in making your journey so much easier, but more is required to become who we are made to become. Many are educated, but can't get a job, or they are working for a mediocre salary. Get your education but dig deeper for more.
2. It is not always the qualified who are called.
3. It's not a gift to walk in purpose. It is your birthright.
4. Your passion can be turned into wealth.

When I was first approached by some of these people to offer my services, it was nerve-wracking at first. Even now, I sometimes get nervous when I write and send off material for client criticism. I keep imagining them just canceling the job because I wrote rubbish, but that has never happened. To be praised by the learned and well-respected men and women in different parts of the world has been humbling, and I truly understand just how powerful the God who lives inside me really is, and just how filled with potential I am. I also believe I have just scratched the surface of my potential as a human being.

If this book can get you to have dreams as a teenager, and start working toward that, I would have accomplished my assignment. It doesn't matter who you are, or how old you are, God wants to use you to accomplish that thing you have been dreaming about, whether it is a book, music, art, whatever you are passionate about; if you believe enough in your dream and are willing to invest in it, I guarantee you that God will cause you to do great and mighty things that will blow your mind.

Everyone has something in them that God wants to use to impact this world. Believe in yourself and go for it.

I am a published author, ghostwriter, playwright, screenwriter, and publishing guru, and this is just a summarized version of my journey. I have a registered online business, and I just officially launched my publishing company a few months ago. This is my world, and it is an ever-expanding world because God has no limits, so I put no limits on myself because God lives in me.

You have more power than you know. That's just how God made you. He created you in His image and likeness, which means you are more like Him than you are anything else. This may be a contrasting statement to who you are presently, but that can change.

I must first tell you who you are. You cannot apply knowledge you do not know. You must first know who you are.

Then you must believe who you are. Knowledge without active faith is just a burden. Assimilating what you know is the first step to manifesting your desires.

Walk, think, and live in the reality of who you are. Make every decision, build every friendship, and react to every circumstance from that place of knowing who you really are.

Only then can you begin to walk in the reality of who you really are and begin to create a world you will be comfortable living in.

CHAPTER ONE

Power to Choose

Let's begin with a few questions:

- ✦ What kind of world would you like to live in tomorrow?
- ✦ What would you change about the present world around you now?
- ✦ If you could decide your future, what would that look like?

To understand the power you have to make a choice; let's go back to the beginning.

> *In the beginning God created the heavens and the earth. (Genesis 1:1)*

The first verse of the very first chapter of the Bible begins with a choice. God chose to create. Then further on He said:

> "Let Us make man in Our image, according to Our likeness; let them have dominion over the fish of the sea, over the birds of the air, and over the cattle, over all the earth and over every creeping thing that creeps on the earth." (Genesis 1:26)

God made a choice to make man, but, even more so, He made a choice to make a being that had the power to choose — just like Him. You can do anything you want with your life, including rejecting God. So, why are so many people not accepting or believing God? Because they can. They have the power to choose what they want to believe and what they want to do with their lives.

Before there was anything, God chose to create something. Everything created came out of Him, and is sustained by Him, and exists only because of Him. Nothing can exist outside of God.

When He made man, He also put within us that same ability to choose. Everything externally that has been created by man was initially a thought or an idea and was manifested because somebody made a choice to pull something from an unseen realm into the realm of the seen. This ability to choose is inbuilt, and it functions from your power to make a choice. You decide what to manifest, and what not to manifest. You create the world you live in, by the choices you make.

The challenge you face is to choose rightly, which is far more difficult than it sounds. If you have ever been addicted to anything, for example, sex, drugs, or masturbation, then you know how hard it is to choose right. Yet, our reality is dependent on our choices.

Information derived from internet sources claim that an adult makes up to 35,000 decisions each day. It sounds like a high number, but considering that our brain receives over 400 billion bits of information per second—though it only utilizes a small amount—making thousands of decisions daily may not be too far from the truth. Our lives are built on the decisions we make, and every waking moment demands a choice.

Let's look at two biblical examples of properly utilizing the power of choice. Paul says:

> *And do not **be** conformed to this world, but **be** transformed by the renewing of your mind, that you may prove what is that good and acceptable and perfect will of God. (Romans 12:2)*

This is only possible by will or by choice. Only a human being with the capacity to choose can 'be' something. Our ability to choose causes us to 'become.'

The world functions under its own systems, but we are told not to **BE** conformed to it, denoting a choice. We can choose to **BE** different; and create our own system under which we function. Transformation, therefore, comes by choice.

The second example is:

> *Finally, brethren, whatever things are true, whatever things are noble, whatever things are just, whatever things are pure, whatever things are lovely, whatever things are of good report, if there is any virtue and if there is anything praiseworthy – meditate on these things. (Philippians 4:8)*

You get to choose what you look at; what you focus on; what you think about. Whatever you focus on will multiply in your life, so if you want goodness to multiply in your life, that's where your focus needs to be. If you focus on negative stuff, you will multiply that in your life, and I know you don't want to do that.

ACTIVATION

Start today by focusing on the decisions you make each moment of every day. Ask yourself:

1. Is this what I really want for my life?
2. Do I want to see this multiplied in my life?
3. How will this decision affect others?

4. When my children grow up and reach my age, would I want them doing this?

There are some decisions that others may try to make for you. For example, how you dress, which school you should attend, which church should you go to, the kind of friends you should have, etc. But, ultimately, how those decisions impact your life will depend heavily on what you decide.

The final decision about which direction your life takes is in your hands. So, choose wisely, and measure your decisions against the kind of world you desire to create for yourself.

CHAPTER TWO

Power to Believe

No one on earth or in heaven can force you to believe what you don't want to believe. This is a power you have. You can believe anything you want to believe.

Belief is at the foundation of our existence, and it helps to frame the reality of the world we live in. It also influences how we see and what we hear.

I have taught Bible Study and delivered a few sermons, and I can tell you that challenging people's belief system feels like an impossible mission. But, no one can change without first changing what they believe. Transformation is impossible without a shift in your belief system. A young man who is convinced that a life of crime is his only option of survival will act accordingly. If we can convince him to change what he does, eventually he will fall right back into his old patterns because his belief did not change. If you really want to change somebody, you must address their belief.

No one can take this power away from you, because it's a work of the heart.

> *Keep your heart with all diligence, for out of it spring the issues of life. (Proverbs 4:23)*

All your experiences in life will fall into this category called "the issues of life." There is a suggestion here that everything you face in this life originates and flows from the belief of your hearts. It is the power to believe and the power to choose at work in those who commit the most dastardly acts. We become victims of robbery, abuse, trauma, accidents, etc. because others use this power in a negative way. This also confirms that your belief and choices impact the world around you. It is never just about you.

So, here's a troublesome verse for you:

> *Therefore I say to you, whatever things you ask when you pray, believe that you receive them, and you will have them. (Mark 11:24)*

According to this verse, believing should be enough to manifest that thing you are praying about. But believing is not enough. If you look closely at the text, there are three principles at work (we discuss all three in this book): thought, emotion, and faith. If we unify all three into one single focus, we can manifest our heart's desire. Because most of us were brought up in such a negative environment, we easily use these three principles to manifest negative stuff. This is why you don't feel worthy, you don't put any value on yourself, and you may be thinking your life has no meaning.

You must learn to use thought, emotion, and faith to manifest God's goodness in your life—His love, prosperity, and health. Think of this as cultivating a field. You cannot reap what you do not sow. You must learn to plant what you want to reap for yourself, and your future family.

The power to believe, if used correctly, can begin to cultivate a field of limitless possibilities in your life.

ACTIVATION

Examine your heart. The goal is to identify what you believe. It would be a good idea to start a journal at this stage in your life. That is where you can record thoughts that may not be easily articulated at this stage in your life, but it's good to keep a record of your progress.

You want to identify your belief system. Answer these questions truthfully:

1. What do you believe about yourself? Was your life a mistake? Do you feel like your life has meaning?

2. What do you believe about your parents? Do they love you? Are they showing genuine concern for your life? Do they speak positively into your life?

3. What do you believe about church? Are they meeting your needs? Do they challenge you to be a better person?

4. What do you believe about your friends? Are they positive or negative influences? Do they really love you for who you are presently?
5. Do you ever have to put on a mask and pretend so you can be comfortable around anyone in your life?
6. What do you genuinely believe about God?

Your heart carries many secrets; some are hidden from even you. To probe the depths of your heart, you must learn to ask the right questions. Your heart can believe a lie, but it will never lie to you.

CHAPTER THREE

Power to Speak

So far, we have talked about the Power to Choose and the Power to Believe. The next one we will discuss is the Power to Speak. You will notice that with all three of these attributes, while other people can influence how they function, you have total control over them. They were given to you, and only you have the responsibility to cultivate them so they function the way they should. These are the facilities given to you by God as a co-creator. Directly, or indirectly, they help to shape and form the life you live now, and in the future.

Let's start this chapter on a good note:

> *You will also declare a thing, and it will be established for you; so light will shine on your ways. (Job 22:28)*

To *'declare'* is to speak, and the word *'established'* suggests that what you speak will be made known or come into existence. That is powerful, and you have this power in your mouth. The problem is, it goes both ways:

> *Death and life are in the power of the tongue, and those who love it will eat its fruit. (Proverbs 18:22)*

My goal is not to scare you but to empower you. I know you may have never heard just how powerful you are as a person, so I want to drive that home so you can change the world. Every single time you open your mouth, you either create life or you create death.

The physical world that you can see with your natural eyes is just one dimension, and it's not complex. In essence, what you see is what you get. The spiritual dimension, however, is far more complex, and a lot of unseen activity goes on there. I am not talking about a cosmic battle between angels and demons. I am talking about how you affect that dimension by thought, belief, spoken words, and action. You can speak a word that changes something in your physical environment without even making the connection, because the words you speak impact the dimension you cannot see, and everything in the physical realm flows from there.

I listen to how people talk and what they say, and it's of great concern. We have cultivated a language of death and not life. We speak negatively about others, always focusing on their weaknesses and mistakes, and not seeing how our words affect them from a spiritual perspective. I believe we make people sick by gossiping about them and stabbing them in the back. You may be happy to hear this because some people in your life deserve to be sick, from your perspective, but remember, you will always sow what you reap. Human beings are so connected that you can't hurt another person without hurting yourself somehow. I believe God did this intentionally, which is why we are commanded to forgive.

So, your words are powerful and should be used with caution. It is better to be silent until you learn to speak life.

> *Oh, that you would <u>be silent</u>, and it would be your wisdom! (Job 13:5)*

> *<u>Be silent</u>, all flesh, before the Lord, for He is aroused from His holy habitation! (Zechariah 2:13)*

> *So then, my beloved brethren, let every man be swift to hear, <u>slow to speak</u>, slow to wrath; for the wrath of man does not produce the righteousness of God. (James 1:19-20)*

> *In the multitude of words sin is not lacking, but he who restrains his lips is wise. (Proverbs 10:19)*

It's hard to be a talkative person and not gossip and spread rumors.

If you know you can have whatever you say, would you keep saying the same things you do now?

If you are going to create a better world for yourself and your future generation, then you need to speak it into existence. You must learn to speak the things that are not, as though they already are (Romans 4:17). Your words have power and carry a lot of weight. Use your words wisely and create life and not death.

ACTIVATION

What do you want to see manifest in your life in the area of Family, Career, or Education and Spiritual Life?

Write down ten Declarations in each category.

Each day, try to make these declarations one to two times.

Here are some sample declarations:

I decree and declare that:

I am a child of God

I am filled with the power and grace of God

I walk in that power

I am filled with the fullness of God

His presence fills my being

I am the embodiment of life

Bringing life into creation

I am the joy of the Lord

I am His holiness

My identity is bound up with Him

Out of this identity —

I decree and declare that

My body is healthy

I am love in the deepest essence

My whole being vibrates love

I am a son of God

Love vibrates from inside my being and impacts the world

I live, move, and act in perfect love and total freedom in Christ

Wisdom, Understanding, Counsel, Power, Knowledge, Might, the Fear of the Lord flows around me

I live the life of Christ

I am my Father's confidence, and He is mine

I decree and declare that

I am healthy. I am in good health.

I am prosperous. I am wealthy.

Wealth is attracted to me.

I attract abundance.

I attract money. I attract prosperity.

You can create your own declarations by using these as a template or guide.

CHAPTER FOUR

Power to Imagine

I am now in my early 40s, and I have a few regrets in life. One of which is not learning from a very early age the power of imagination. If you are reading this and you are in your teen years, you have a unique opportunity to revolutionize your life by understanding how to apply the power of imagination.

Imagination is the faculty that God gave us to see beyond the physical dimension. With imagination, you can see everything and create anything.

Like everything else, imagination can be corrupt and can be used in an evil way, but like everything else, imagination can be redeemed and used for good, just the way God intended.

Imagination is the board on which vision is recorded. Most people who have experienced immeasurable success were able to see it long before it became a reality. It is this faculty that keeps you going after your dreams and never giving up. You hold on to the image that you saw of yourself in a certain position, and you go after it.

As I began to learn about the function of imagination, I soon realized that it showed me the future. I would see myself doing certain things, or even getting the answer to some problems just moments before doing what I saw. It is such a remarkable discovery that I started to pay attention to everything that came to my imagination.

No one can tap into the true potential of this ability like you can. Use it to fuel your life, to go after an impossible dream, to excel beyond your own limited thinking. Where reality draws boundaries and says you cannot go beyond them, imagination takes you beyond them. It knows no limits. If there is a part of you that understands the limitlessness of the God who created you, it's your imagination.

Let's examine again this scripture from Chapter Two:

> *Therefore I say to you, whatever things you ask when you pray, believe that you receive them, and you will have them. (Mark 11:24)*

Without imagination, you cannot *"...believe that you receive them..."* This verse could have easily said, *"Imagine that you already have it..."*

Do you want to see the real, unhindered power of your imagination?

> *And the LORD said, Behold, the people is one, and they have all one language; and this they begin to do: and now nothing will be restrained from them, which they have <u>imagined</u> to do. (Genesis 11:6)*

Imagination opens up the world of impossibilities and makes them possible. The people at the Tower of Babel had a thought. They saw themselves building a tower that reached into heaven. If God had not done something, they would have succeeded. The question you must ask is, how were they going to build that tower if there were no bricks, cement, or skyscrapers? The answer is, they would have found a way.

Only people who are ignorant of who they are, and how they are supposed to function, make excuses for why they can't excel at what they do. We are overachievers by nature, especially when it comes to working as a team.

ACTIVATION

Begin to journal your dreams.

Write down the images you see on the screen of your imagination, especially when you are praying.

Your life may not be making sense now, but it will eventually. Avoid missing those defining moments that come in the spur of the moment.

Imagination is the landing place for innovative ideas, business ideas, creative ideas, etc. Any new idea must first be impressed on the imagination before it even stands a chance of manifesting in this physical world. The secular world understands this more than Christians do.

Wouldn't you want to be the first to capture the next revolutionary idea? You can, if you just pay attention to what is happening in your imagination.

Another good practice is to close your eyes and see yourself engaging heavenly dimensions. See yourself entering the throne room of God, bowing before Him in worship. See yourself having moments of conversation with Jesus, asking questions and waiting for a response. I believe this is a good practice in redeeming your imagination to focus on what is good, pure, right, etc.

CHAPTER FIVE

Power to Create

When we were children growing up, we created a lot of things. We made trucks from bottle covers and empty juice boxes, kites from old bags and strings, boats and planes from recycled paper, robots from clay and outdoor huts from grass, sticks, and old bags. It is funny how we understood our roles and power as creators as kids more than when we became adults.

All the amenities we use today were made by man. That includes laptops, cell phones, television, radio, fans, etc. Man created all transportation, i.e., cars, buses, trucks, spaces, and spaceships. It was all conceptualized by a man and built by the hands of men. Even the machines that are replacing manpower in certain circles were built by man. Every building, no matter how majestic it seems, was conceptualized, designed, and built by man. That potential to create resides in everyone, including you.

We have the potential to start businesses, families, build corporations and educational institutions. By nature, we create. The one who seeks only pleasure from life will never fully understand this innate power. It should not be enough to want to utilize what others created. You should seek to be responsible for bringing something from the unseen world into this one, something that will make someone's life easier or be a solution to a problem. That's what life is about.

The preservation of life on the earth is dependent on what you bring to the table. Don't be a consumer of products but also be a replenisher, a creator, a founder, an inventor. You have the potential to do this.

God made you a creator so you can co-labor with Him in making the world a better place. God can do everything we are supposed to do, but He chooses not to. God is not going to make a better plane, or cars that hover and don't use gas but can run on water, or a more innovative laptop or artificial intelligence. You are going to do all that.

The power you have to create makes you an invaluable asset to this world because you have something to offer in making the world a better place. Don't ever accept or believe that you have nothing to offer this world, but must work for somebody. When you work for somebody, you are helping them create their dream. You too have a dream, something that needs to be birthed. This is how we become lenders and not borrowers. As long as you are a borrower, you have not yet tapped into your true potential as a human being.

I write this book particularly with teenagers in mind. I believe the ages of fifteen to eighteen is the perfect time to begin to grasp the ideas presented in this book. If I can help you avoid being a late-bloomer like myself, where I learned valuable life lessons well into my thirties, I would have contributed to making tomorrow a better world for us all.

You have the power to create, so ensure that you choose a career path that lines up with your passion. If you don't know what your passion is, just begin to examine your life and find those things you love to do. Your passion is there somewhere. When you have found your passion, do some research to find careers that would facilitate those passions and pursue along those lines. If you need to start working at a young age to help your family financially, and you find yourself doing menial jobs that you hate, just try to keep your eyes on the prize. Invest some of your earnings toward your dream. Spend on resources and materials you will need to make it happen. Be persistent and never give up on finding your path in life. You will know when you get there because it will be the most rewarding and fulfilling time in your life.

ACTIVATION

What are you passionate about?

There are some things you do that you really love doing. That's where you need to look. It could be sports, music, art, etc. It is important to find your passion because, very often, your purpose is tied to it.

If money was not an issue, and you could create one thing that would either make life easier or solve a problem, what would that be?

Write your answer down somewhere. The fact that you can even conceive of this is an indication that it may very well be one of your life's assignment.

CHAPTER SIX

Power to Feel

Emotions have been mostly misunderstood, and it is necessary to understand who you are as an emotional being, to affect change.

Emotions are not unimportant, because they play a key role in changing the world around you. The mistake we make is that we spend so much time cultivating negative emotions that we fail to use it properly to create good. It's easy to focus on what is wrong with people. We tend to see the glass as half empty and not half full. We see people's sin and not their hearts or motives. We talk about people in a negative light; backstabbing, backbiting, gossiping, and spreading all kinds of rumors—even though we profess to hate when this is done to us. And we do all this from an emotional perspective. We are guilty of the very things we hate for people to do to us, so we end up judging others but not realizing that we also judge ourselves.

It feels good to destroy someone's reputation, and if you follow your emotions, you may even be convinced that you are doing the world a favor. The problem is, you are made to carry light, love, and life into the world, not death. Part of you will feel good when putting down others. It causes you to feel better about yourself, as if your sins are not that bad compared to him or her. If you are going to be a world changer, you cannot function at this level.

Emotions also play a part in how we feel about ourselves.

- *Do you believe you have self-worth?*
- *Do you value yourself?*
- *How important are you to the world around you?*

We often measure these by how we feel, which is not accurate most of the time, because a skewed emotional predisposition is not a good judge of your value and worth. This is why we often hear people say, *"I feel worthless"* or *"I feel inadequate."* Feeling it doesn't make it true. You only feel that way because you have trained your emotions negatively, or the circumstances around you have highly influenced how you feel.

I'm not saying that having bad experiences doesn't matter. You may have been abused, molested, or raped. You could have made some terrible choices—fornication, getting pregnant, and having an abortion. These are all real experiences that influence emotion, but they should not be used to define you.

Feelings cannot be trusted to determine outcomes and responses, unless you have done the work to cultivate more positive emotions. One of the worse things we do in church is use feelings to determine the spiritual atmosphere.

Cultivating positive emotions requires effort, commitment, and persistence to work through all the junk and find our true emotional center. If you can do this and pair your positive emotion with thought and declaration, you can change atmospheres; you can change the world. What happens in this place is that you find that all your desires, which will now be cultivated from a positive place, will begin to manifest in and around your life.

> *Delight yourself also in the Lord, and He shall give you the desires of your heart. (Psalm 37:4)*

"Delight" is a very strong emotion. It is finding enjoyment, pleasure, happiness, joy, and glee in the Lord. Our pleasure should not come from sin. You must find that place in God where you derive satisfaction from Him and nothing else. If you can function emotionally from that place, all your desires will be met. Our **Father is always willing to give the world to a happy child.**

Another powerful emotion is love. I am not convinced that even our traditional churches have learned to love each other as we should. There is a lot of judgment in church, and we are quick to judge people by their mistakes and not by what God thinks of them. As a church, we have not represented God well emotionally, and it has done more damage than we are willing to admit.

> *There is no fear in love; but perfect love casts out fear, because fear involves torment. But he who fears has not been made perfect in love. (1 John 4:18)*

Love is the antidote for fear. The presence of fear suggests an absence of love.

> *And above all things have fervent love for one another, for "love will cover a multitude of sins." (1 Peter 4:8)*

Love is a powerful emotion, but it is also a choice. I am about to say something that you have never heard before. The power to choose is intimately linked with our emotion. You can choose how and what you feel. If this was not possible, then it would not be possible to be angry and not sin. It would not be possible to be silent when you really want to speak, and it would not be possible to suppress your emotions.

The power to feel plays a vital role in our responsibility as creators. The challenge is to train yourself to feel good about the right things so you can transform your environment to demonstrate the "goodness of God."

ACTIVATION

What makes you feel good?

This may seem like a trick question because not everything that makes you feel good is good. Sin can feel good, but it can have a terrible impact on your conscience. So, the feel-good effect is not long-lived.

God didn't create humanity for sin, so it will never be satisfying, no matter how much our conscience is seared.

What are some of the most dominant emotions in your everyday life?

If you can identify these, it will help identify your strengths and passions as well.

For example, if you get angry easily, then find out what angers you. Sometimes your intolerance of something can help you see what you really appreciate in life.

Finally, and this is the most difficult; *in the height of feeling a strong emotion, sit down in a quiet place, close your eyes, and try to*

manipulate your emotions. See if you can change how you feel in that moment. It can happen with just a shift in thought, but with practice, you can learn how to feel different, even without thought.

CHAPTER SEVEN

Power to Know

Have you ever heard the saying, "Knowledge is Power?" Well, it is partially true. Knowledge without application will not produce anything in your life. It is not enough just to gather information.

I was talking with one of my young protégés a few years ago about preaching. He said, *"I can't preach."* He had never attempted to preach, so I understood why he would think that. However, he is an excellent cook and a superb cake maker. So, I asked him, *"How did you learn how to cook?"* He had received quite a bit of theoretical knowledge in college, but that doesn't make you a cook, just as my theoretical journey as a carpenter did not make me one.

You learn to cook by cooking. You also learn by making mistakes and trying to correct them. You should hear that young man preach today.

Transformation is a practical journey, and if this book is going to benefit you at all, you must practice these principles. Otherwise, it's just more information taking up cognitive space in your brain that will not change your life in any way. And if you don't change, you cannot change anyone.

So, I am not discrediting knowledge. You need to know, and you have the power to know. Knowledge is available, if you want it. Thousands of books are being published every day on every topic conceivable. Whatever interest you have, you can find a book about it.

Sadly, if you don't read, you are going to miss a great deal of personal transformation and revelation needed to catapult you into greatness.

ACTIVATION

The first thing you want to do is ***find some books on topics that interest you*** and begin to read. If you are not a reader, take it slowly and take it in strides. Do a chapter a week, two pages a day, whatever pace is comfortable for you. Highlight phrases that stand out in your mind and take notes. Seek practical methods you can apply to your life, short and long term. This is important for your own growth and development.

The next step is to **utilize YouTube.** I have an interest in Christian Mysticism, so I find all the modern day Christian Mystics and listen to all their messages and teachings, and I read all their books. In the past few years, I have listened to over 3000 hours of teaching from my mentor.

So, for example, if photography is your passion, find the best in the field and follow and learn from them.

FINAL THOUGHTS

Most of you probably hate the world you live in. But maybe nobody ever told you that you had the power to change it. Only you can change your world and make it a better one.

There are things I don't want you to forget.

1. *You will always reap from what you sow.* Try to cultivate a field of good thoughts, emotions, and spoken word so you will reap a harvest of goodness.
2. *Your circumstances don't define you, so stop spending so much time looking at the past.* I know you may have been hurt badly, and it's hard to forgive and move on, but your greater you is in the future, not the past. Draw as much as you can from your future, utilizing the gift of imagination, and forget your past.

3. ***Nobody knows you better than the One who created you.*** Listen to Him. He speaks to you, whether you are a Christian or not. One of the voices you hear inside belongs to Him. You can't go wrong if you learn to identify that voice and believe what He says enough to walk in obedience.

4. ***You have great value and self-worth.*** You were chosen from a pool of a million possibilities, so you are extremely special. If you don't believe that now, you have a lot of work to do. Don't settle for mediocrity or feelings of worthlessness, or you will create a world for yourself and your future family that neither of you will like. Because of humanity's connectedness, your decisions affect more than just you.

5. ***You can be anything you want to be.*** God put this potential inside every human being born in this world. It doesn't matter what the color of your skin is, your social status, your address, or environment, or even the circumstances that brought you here; you have the power to rise above it all. You were made to be great.

The world waited a long time for you to get here. Creation celebrated your birth. You have the potential, the capacity, and the power to create a better world. Why would you want to do otherwise?

Love this Book?

Connect with me:

Instagram: @cleveland.mcleish

Facebook: @hcpbookpublishing
@ authorcorvillemcleish

Email: **info@hcpbookpublishing.com**
cleveland.mcleish@gmail.com

Website: **www.hcpbookpublishing.com**
www.madeingodsimage.blog